ON THE FARM

MACHINES

Warren Singer

Enslow PUBLISHING

Published in 2026 by Enslow Publishing, LLC
2544 Clinton Street
Buffalo, NY 14224

First Published 2025 by Redback Publishing

Author: Warren Singer
Editors: Lucinda Dodds and Emma Dobinson
Designer: Redback Publishing
Original illustrations © Redback Publishing 2025
Originated by Redback Publishing

Acknowledgements
Abbreviations: l—left, r—right, b—bottom,
t—top, c—centre, m—middle
We would like to thank the following for permission to reproduce photographs:
Shutterstock; 13tl ChameleonsEye / Shutterstock.com, 21tl Steve Jolicoeur / Shutterstock.com, 21mr Leanne Irwin / Shutterstock.com, 23b Nalidsa / Shutterstock.com, 26b Serge Goujon / Shutterstock.com

Manufactured in the United States of America

CPSIA compliance information: Batch #CSENS26: For further information contact Enslow Publishing LLC, New York, New York at 1-800-398-2504.

Please visit our website, www.enslowpublishing.com.
For a free color catalog of all our high-quality books,
call toll free 1-800-398-2504 or fax 1-877-980-4454.

Cataloging-in-Publication Data
Names: Singer, Warren.
Title: Machines / Warren Singer.
Description: Buffalo, NY : Enslow Publishing, 2026. |
Series: On the farm | Includes glossary and index.
Identifiers: ISBN 9781978546073 (pbk.) |
ISBN 9781978546080 (library bound) | ISBN 9781978546097 (ebook)
Subjects: LCSH: Agricultural machinery--Juvenile literature. | Farms--Juvenile literature.
Classification: LCC S675.25 S564 2026 | DDC 631.3--dc23

Find us on

CONTENTS

MIGHTY MACHINES

How many big machines does it take to make just one ice cream in a cone?

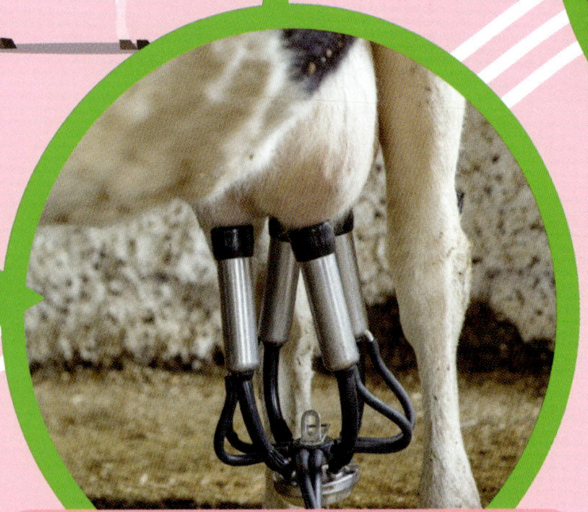

MILKING MACHINE

Milk comes from cows.

STEEL VATS

The milk is collected and stored.

MILK TANKER

Big trucks take milk to the factory.

THE MILK IS HEATED

The heat kills germs in the milk.

SCIENTISTS TEST THE MILK

They make sure it is safe to drink.

THE MILK IS PUT INTO CONTAINERS AND SOLD

People buy milk to drink, but factories also buy milk to make different foods.

ICE CREAM FACTORIES FREEZE THE MILK AND CREAM

They also add colors and flavors.

THE ICE CREAM TRAVELS TO STORES IN TRUCKS

The trucks have to be cold so the ice cream does not melt.

YOU BUY IT AND ENJOY IT!

HARVESTERS

Huge fields of wheat or other grains are too big for a person to harvest without the help of big machines.

Some harvesting machines are 16 feet (5 m) high, and 36 feet (11 m) long. That's about the size of a double-decker bus!

A combine harvester makes work much easier for the farmer. It cuts the wheat seeds from the fields and gets rid of the dry, outer covering of the seed, called the chaff.

The farmers need just the wheat seeds to store and sell.

FACT

It takes 10 square feet (1 sq m) of wheat plants to make a small loaf of bread.

FACT

The biggest wheat farms in the world are in China.

MILKING MACHINES

Farmers in the past milked cows by hand. Now farmers use milking machines.

The machines do not harm the cows. A whole herd of cows will line up, waiting to be milked every day.

Robot milking machines do not need a farmer to be there when the cows are being milked. The machines do all the work.

In the future, machines run by computer programs will be used more and more to milk large herds of dairy cows.

FACT
The biggest milking machines can milk thousands of cows at once.

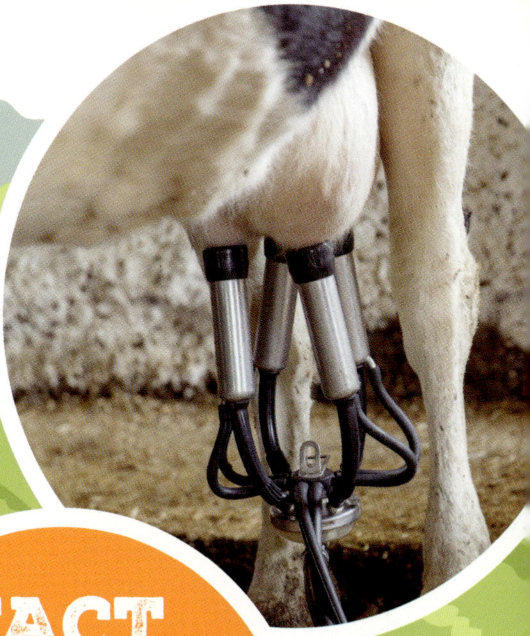

FACT
Some milking sheds are bigger than a football field.

IRRIGATORS

A farmer cannot water a vast crop with just a hose! Some farmers use motorized irrigators. Some of these machines move by themselves across a field.

Pivot irrigators do not move along a field. Instead, they spray water around in a circle. The arms on this machine can be hundreds of feet long.

The irrigator can pump its water from a channel that the farmer has to dig beside the fields. Some farmers pump water from underground.

In places with low rainfall, farmers rely on using irrigators to keep their crops alive.

FACT

An irrigator is a machine that sprays water onto a field.

FACT

A moving irrigator can be thousands of feet long.

SUGAR TRAINS

Special sugar trains take the sugarcane from the large fields to a factory.

The railway lines for sugarcane trains are not used for ordinary passengers. Their only purpose is to carry sugarcane.

On some farms, trucks and other road vehicles have replaced sugar trains, though many rail systems are still used today.

FACT

A sugar train can be 0.6 mile (1 km) long.

FACT

Sugar comes from sugarcane that farmers grow in fields.

DID YOU KNOW?

Sugarcane is actually a type of giant grass.

TRACTORS

Farmers have to move heavy loads all around their farms. They rely on tractors to help them get the work done.

Tractors pull trailers loaded with animals, hay, harvested crops, and wood and stone for building on the farm. Tractors also pull other heavy machines.

Tractors can have round wheels, or they might be fitted with tracks. A track fits around more than one wheel and helps the tractor grab the ground safely.

FACT

Before tractors were invented, farmers used animals such as horses and oxen to pull heavy loads.

FACT

Some farms use automated tractors. Future tractors may be able to predict crop needs and self-repair.

DID YOU KNOW?

Toy tractors are one of the most popular toys in the world, even with children who have never seen a farm or a real tractor.

ROBOTS AND FRUIT

Nearly all fruit is picked by people, but they may not be needed to do this job in the future. Robots will be able to do it more quickly and in any sort of weather.

Computer engineers are playing an important role on farms by designing robots that can pick fruit without crushing it.

Fruit-picking robots have cameras in them that look at the fruit. The computer program then decides if the fruit looks ripe or not.

The robot has to hold the fruit tightly enough not to drop it, but not so tightly that the fruit is ruined.

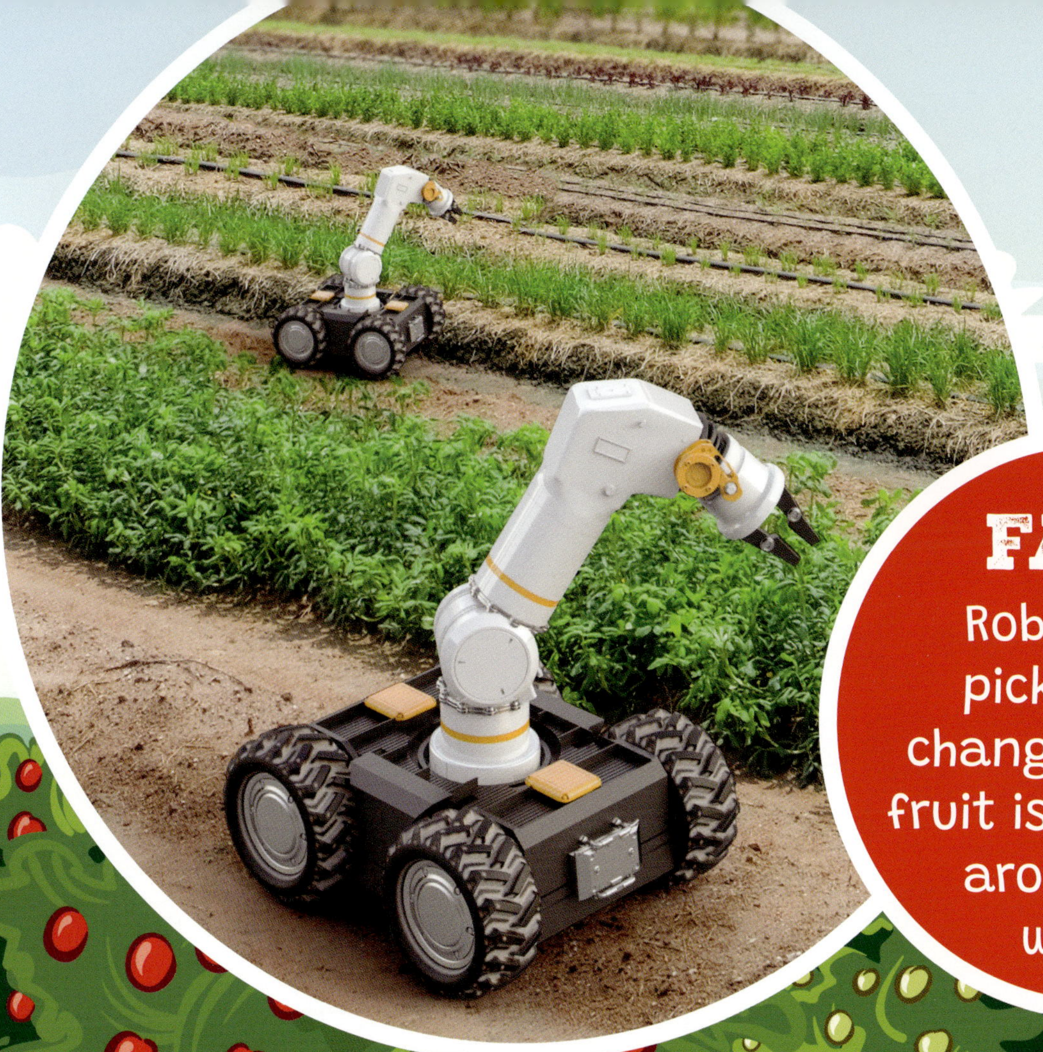

FACT

Robot fruit pickers will change the way fruit is harvested around the world.

FACT

The cost of farm robots is very high, so only the largest farms can use them.

DAIRY FACTORY

Milk has to go through a factory before it gets poured into the bottles or cartons you buy at the supermarket.

Bottling machines fill thousands of bottles every day, but the milk has to be checked before it leaves the factory.

Scientists work in dairy factories. They check the milk for germs that would make people sick.

Cheese, yogurt, cream, ice cream, and butter all come from milk. In factories, these foods are made with large machines.

FACT

Spray drying turns milk into a dry powder that is sold in cans in stores.

FACT

A centrifuge spins the milk around to separate the cream.

SILOS

When farmers harvest large amounts of grain, such as wheat or corn, they cannot send it straight to a factory to be made into food. They first store the grain in massive silos.

If you see these tall cylinders on farmland, you might wonder what could be inside. You would be surprised to see the silos hold billions of grains.

The silos keep the grain safe from the weather, and from mice and insects. That is why silos are mostly made from metal or concrete, with no gaps where pests can get into them.

The silos have machinery to move the grain in and out, and from one spot to another. Modern silos are operated by computers.

FACT

Grain in silos can explode into a fire if not stored properly.

FACT

Sometimes people paint silos, making beautiful art.

ATVs

ATV is short for "all-terrain vehicle." Farmers use ATVs to ride around their farm, to inspect fences, or to check on animals.

ATVs have four wheels that are wider than the wheels on an ordinary motorbike. This makes ATVs easier to ride over rough ground.

ATVs have replaced horse riding for many jobs around the farm, like rounding up livestock that need to be moved into a fenced area.

FACT

Farm dogs learn to jump up onto the ATV so they can ride with the farmer.

FACT

An ATV is also called a quad bike.

FARM AIRCRAFT

In countries such as Australia, Canada, and the United States, where the farms can be as big as small countries, farmers pilot small aircraft to get around their farms.

From up high, farmers can see where lost animals are hiding. They can also check on the condition of the pastures.

Helicopters are used to muster cattle. They can hover in the one spot so are better for working with livestock than planes are.

Drones are the newest sort of aircraft that farmers are using to inspect their farms by looking down on them from up high.

FACT
Drones are saving lives, as being an agricultural pilot can be dangerous.

FACT
Killing bugs by dropping pesticides from aircraft is called crop dusting.

ROAD TRAINS

Road trains are an important way to transport cattle and produce in places where there are not enough railways to cover the whole country. They are not used in the United States.

A powerful truck can pull up to four trailers creating a convoy that can be over 165 feet (50 m) long. Some of the road trains have two levels.

Once one of these long road trains reaches a city, the trailers have to be divided up and attached to separate trucks so they can get around corners on a suburban street.

FACT
A road train full of cattle leaves a smell behind it that lingers for a long time.

FACT
Australia has the longest road trains in the world. They can be as long as two basketball courts.

WINDMILLS

In some parts of the world, windmills use the power of wind to turn machinery that pumps water up from underground. The water then pours into a dam or a container where animals can come to drink.

In the Netherlands, windmills pump water away from farms to stop them from flooding.

Modern windmills are built to provide electricity for people in cities as well as on farms.

FACT

Windmills are an ancient way to generate power from the wind.

FACT

In the past, millers used a windmill to turn a heavy grinding stone for crushing wheat into flour for bread.

TANKERS

Tankers are large trucks with long, rounded tanks at the back used for carrying liquids or gases. Milk is transported from farms to dairy factories in tankers.

Some tankers carry oil that has been squeezed out of plants so that it can be used for cooking. The oil has to be taken to factories to be put into bottles or containers and then sold.

Tankers also carry water, wine from vineyards, liquid sugar, or even honey.

Food tankers have to be cleaned very well before and after each load is transported.

FACT

Food tankers look like gas tankers, but one can never be swapped with the other.

FACT

Food tankers are filled from a hole in the top but emptied from a pipe at the bottom.

GLOSSARY

Mighty Farm Machines

centrifuge ....machine that spins to separate contents of a liquid

chaff ....dry, outer parts of seeds

channel ....trench to carry water

dairy foods ....foods made from milk

harvest ....to bring in a crop or pick fruit

hay ....dry grasses used for livestock food

herd ....group of cows

muster ....gather animals together

oxen ....cattle kept by farmers to do work

vat ....large storage tub for liquids

INDEX